THE KINGDOM

Jane Draycott was born in London and is the author of eight collections of poetry and poetic translation, including *No Theatre* (Smith/Doorstop, Forward Prizes shortlist) and *Prince Rupert's Drop* (Forward Prize for Best Collection shortlist), *Over* (T.S. Eliot Prize shortlist) and *The Occupant* (PBS Recommendation), all from Carcanet Press. A 2004 Next Generation poet, her several awards include a Stephen Spender Prize for her Carcanet translation of the medieval dream-elegy *Pearl*, as well as the Keats Shelley Prize for Poetry and the Hippocrates Prize for Poetry and Medicine. Her collaborative work includes, with poet Lesley Saunders and artist Peter Hay, two illustrated collections *Christina the Astonishing* and *Tideway*, both re-issued from Two Rivers Press in 2022. She teaches on postgraduate writing programmes at the universities of Oxford and Lancaster and is a Fellow of the Royal Society of Literature.

The Kingdom

JANE DRAYCOTT

CARCANET POETRY

First published in Great Britain in 2022 by
Carcanet
Alliance House, 30 Cross Street
Manchester, M2 7AQ
www.carcanet.co.uk

A CIP catalogue record for this book is
available from the British Library.

ISBN 978 1 80017 259 3

Book design by Andrew Latimer
Printed in Great Britain by SRP Ltd, Exeter, Devon

The publisher acknowledges financial
assistance from Arts Council England.

CONTENTS

for Norman, Holly and Sophie

THE OTHERS

Arriving last (having furthest
    to travel) I asked the others
what brink or brim this was
    – the world under water,
the flood itself flooded
    with sun like a rift-valley lake
from which flamingoes
    might lift as if from an ark

the whole affair pressed
    with a luminous inverted cloud-map
like the other side of a coin
    that fell once from pocket
to market-place floor, an unobserved
    loss revealed centuries later
not face-down in the mud
    but gazing up skywards –

the greatest wonder of all being
    how they had called me there,
the others, how I'd moved so much
    further away than I thought,
how I might not have surfaced at all.

THE KINGDOM

I was hungry
    coming up from Kent
resorting hyther after the summer

my tent a riverbed
    seeking herbergement
some accommodation among the stone

the men coming on to you
  the taxi drivers saying here jump in no
    no you don't need no money.

I was thirsty
      languissyng in the doorway
behind the post office

the churchyard water
    so cold for washing
– what eyleth thee woman? –

and from my mouth came leaves
and from the cracks in the pavement
    came syllables.

I was a stranger
   turned half to stone
seeking releyf in severe weather

coming hyther in search of something
    oute of thys madnesse
something to inherit.

THE CLAIM

So many came to that portion
of the claim, the water not too deep there,
and left with tiny grains of gold,

dust really, and the freezing work
painstaking to the bone,
all that remained of Eldorado

like the land of how-to videos
we'd flocked to, so much
we'd hoped that could be fixed,

the shattered screen,
the damaged heat-pump like a heart
destroyed by years of insults

even, one mountebank declared,
the mind, split into a dozen pieces
like a priceless vase exploded

on a marble floor, slipped
from the aristocrat's hands
(the crane in flight, the little bridge,

the homeward labourers as snow
begins to fall). In the ancient art
of the broken all could be repaired

with shining seams of precious metal,
the bird, the village and the snow,
and even made more lovely

by the gleaming scars. All you needed
was sufficient gold. All you needed
was to not be finished by the cold.

SOME CHILDREN

would only sleep with the windows
wide open as if lying under the stars
or out in the street,
                                couldn't settle except
with a breeze coming in (occasional
hailstones, stray bullet-fire, bricks),

were afraid they'd lose part of themselves
in the black-out
                        so they lay there alert
for the sound of the adults safely back
from the dark, for the hooves of the horses

that leapt from the paintings downstairs
to roam with the foxes and night birds,
all the souls who'd been turned into trees.

Every infant kept vigil, awake
and on the *qui-vive:* who goes there,
what is that company out there?

OUR TOWN AND THE FALCON

This is roomy country, and not
just from the air:
          down here in town now
we've all got several streets each
to ourselves.
          I like to walk
the place at dawn, as if I were
the only person left on the planet –

our resurfaced car park OUT ONLY,
our new public toilets built
to resemble a small alpine chalet,

our hangars and school halls, cleared
but for the rolls of decommissioned
razor wire. Authorized arrivals
only, lots of room
          for the individual.

We have emptied our hearts
and minds. Feelings rush
towards us from the vacant sky,
bits of asteroid
          rush towards us

homing in like a falcon bringing
fresh new evidence of how
          this could all have begun.

We are preparing to meet
that incoming space dust in every
possible way we can think of.

AT THIS LATITUDE

Polar day is such a magical time. People walk
by the lake together until late, enjoying the warmth

and the golden light. Sometimes it's hard to sleep,
even in imperfect surrender, but people

are happy and the light is so golden together out late
by the lake. Polar night creeps in slowly like a discreet

arresting officer, till one morning round coffee time
you understand there will be no more light

until next year, like climbing alone into an MRI scanner,
the cold slicing through you like meat at the deli counter,

the fear that the sun will never return. Time passes
into a blender. People grow feral. It's hard

not to let the bitter winds take you. Is it wrong to resist,
to desire to live elsewhere than this?

IN THEIR PLATOONS

By midnight when it was all over
        there was no-one, just the woods moving

in their platoons at the edges of the fields
        signalling to each other with their leaf-action.

No more tree-hugging or healing,
        no more sushi chains,

no more psychological thrillers,
        no more where is my husband.

At last they had the place to themselves
        and in their branchy arms

the entire future to optimise –
        birds, rainfall, the next new myths.

THE CIRCLE

In the circle one of the girls said
before this I was an accountant
and a vase
                and we knew
what she meant – something like
a multi-purpose function room
or how in a buffeting wind
                a tree is also
a ritual lion-dance performance.

Then the facilitator said so let's
consider the relationship between a piece
        of pottery and the maternal womb

but the girl replied no that's not it
more like isn't that amazing
        to be two things at once

like in the middle ages when bread
on the tongue was also the body
                and wine was the blood
and no fuss was made

because though you can count
the number of gates to the heavenly city
and be sure any storm will turn
        your small vessel to matchwood

of our fates we know actually nothing
and some seas might also be lakes
        with another encircling shore to set down on.

THE STREAMING

I heard it faintly and cutting down an alley
near the metro passed through its narrow air
as close as skin – like sky that enters through
an open window – to find your disused mobile
ringing there, propped beneath a dusty tree.
Your voice sounded so near, the line
as clear as if you were beside me on a plane,
almost something fictitious though the tree
bore witness, roots and ribs networking
earth and air. Where was that elsewhere
you were calling from, or did I call you?
Then came the rain, wild, unrestrained
and ominous, its glassy strands descending
through the undermiles of conduits
to the lightless ocean bed. I saw the phone,
I saw my hand. Where there'd been skin
was now a web of ivy heading for my heart.
It seemed a long way back then – the alley's
open window, the chance to be like sky again,
to cast my cloudless eye across the world,
see nothing but its wide and lovely surfaces.

THIS LOVELESS LIBRARY

Such suspect letters for security are piled
        into despatch vans there to slide and sidle
as if huddling on a freezing mountainside

before arriving at this loveless library
        half-eaten by the tireless tides
to here remain unopened, silent

as the trees that fall unheard except by sky
        and earth. Each day I sit among them, trying
to hear the trees, the untold stories of their lives.

MARATHON

Across this field   the farmer's left a track
for you to race down   sky wheat sky
far hedges   banks of remedies
a corridor you run   each visiting night
to see her   nil by mouth no flowers

Around you   in the tumbling air
the plants   secure their future lives
as down the hollow-way   its leafy tracts
and ducts you run   through double doors
to raise funds   catch a person leaving

You'd run for years   if need be
x-ray penicillin x-ray   this sea of corn
you'd swim it like Leander   there and back
each evening   guided by the light beam
at her window   laser chemo laser

outpaced at last   by racing winds
the lamp extinguished   questions still
to ask   why all the dust the flies
what are your reasons for running

THE GLOVES

Mrs Dalloway said she would buy the gloves herself
            'Mrs Dalloway in Bond Street' — V. Woolf, 1923

Some days were long and up to the elbow,
a mix of polyester silk and cloud cover,

sunless but still offering something,
protection for the delicate wrist-parts of the mind

so that as we walked the city, masonry
falling around us, tears rising to our eyes,

sap rose also to our fingertips, and though
no bees or butterflies settled on our palms

leaf buds burst through the stitching,
papery new skins of delphiniums,

sweet peas, irises blossoming, saving us
from arriving at evening empty-handed again.

THE YARD

Tethered as we were to the yard
of the city, something still lifted inside us
till we were so filled up that fire caught

and we were aloft, the balloon-silk doming
over our heads as in our ears the spirits
of the guy-ropes cried out and split.

No sound then but the roar of the burner flames
as we rose past the counter-fall of offices
and treeless gardens, our childhoods

emerging backwards as we floated above
the playgrounds where on Fridays
the police had patrolled with their horses,

until at last the air froze around us, and all
we wanted was to lie again on the warm earth
in the park, listening to the roots of the grass,

like returning sailors rounding the corner
to the last street before home,
thinking already about that other life at sea.

ALONE THAT DAY, I DROVE, THOUGHT

nobody owns that running life up there
          paused now and flowering
like a 3D print of blood and bone.
          Driving on, I felt the arrow-thought:
perhaps that deer was you, survived
          the rifle or the latest vehicle-deer
collision, returned to fix my phone
          or be a virtual deer to battle loneliness.

Later in the twenty streets of town
          I saw it there again, more like
a wolf now standing at the intersection –
          the new free zone, no lights or lines
to stop a speeding car, like butter
          to a bullet. I wished I knew
what it had learned there in the woods.
          I wished I knew if it was me or you.

BEHIND CLOSED DOORS

This profession requires an unruffled temper...
                          Titian, d. 1556 of plague

Night in the nation's gallery,
an avenue of over-branching canvases
walked only by security:

Andromeda in chains, Callisto
exiled to the silent universe – the gods,
their overworld, their club.

Outside, contagion's on the streets
again, bent on self-replication. Tomorrow
they'll let us enter one by one,

insist we keep our distance as Actaeon
might have learned who strayed too near
Diana, perfect android, immortal machine.

Not something he could have imagined,
an afternoon in the forest, his flesh
transformed, his body overtaken.

THE LITTLE CAR AND THE ATTIC

We understood, my good friend and I,
that the little car had taken us into a new epoch
        'La petite auto': Guillaume Apollinaire, d. 1918 of influenza

Just the two of us, our last journey home
and in the headlights the early mist, its fever
of droplets clinging to the flagpoles on the esplanade.

Then inland, white swans on the placid ponds
as we drove through, the sun and the wind
and behind us the miles of sleepless sea.

By afternoon so many eras had passed –
in the fields a profusion of poppies, in the villages
swans the colour of charcoal, children

born with it in their bloodstream
playing at the crossroads, all the evidence
still hanging like rags from the branches.

At dusk we arrived in the city, its botanic gardens
and laboratories, its overflowing hospitals,
each of us wondering how long our luck would last,

climbing the stairs to the attic, thinking we heard
someone down there calling our name.

CALENDAR

Old age came quickly for my frosted generation
        The Garden, Derek Jarman (d.1994 of HIV/AIDS)

My calendar sends notice from the cancelled world:
early tapas then a campfire on the beach with friends.

The parallel hour passes like a bird at night
and waves close over all that's happened there without us,
permanently missing now like Shackleton's lost boat.

Instead I sort the attic, put my hand down through the water
and retrieve your diary, your last: appointments, blood-tests,
drug-trials, anything to save the situation.

The singing too, the days you felt the lovely feeling still.
But nothing marks the long white wilderness
that lay ahead, the ice moving steadily in.

Maybe in the universe that cracked away
you did set foot on solid ground again, perhaps
it's May the sixth today in both our worlds,

the quarter moon, the tides the same,
the same cold constellations in their slow flight by.

IN THE BONES OF THE DISUSED GASOMETER

the domed container would rise, telescoping up…
in the evening the levels would sink back down as the gas
was used to light and heat homes
> Ed Ram: 'Will the UK's gas holders be missed?' BBC 2015

A ruin's a fine thing to swim in, as air does
    in the bones of a disused gasometer,
a chance to think quietly and alone

then climb from the ribs of its municipal
    sky-pool, free from your drowning clothes
and the black wet dog at your heels.

How we lived then with the gas-dragon
    caged out the back between railway
and cricket ground, its nightly reveal

of the roofline, the infirmary lights
    always on like a cruise ship,
the patients pretending to sleep.

Since you've been gone, the pipework's
    been salvaged, reborn as a deep-toning chime
at the opera house where each evening

I sit through the roofless old tale
    of the painter, the lover-like sister, the stain
on the firing squad floor, just to hear it,

continuing life as a nightly-struck bell,
    the derelict stars pouring down
though the holes in the sail of the sky.

SHINE

Electric delta, lily flower, papyrus –
   Alexandria. So sees the night-time satellite,

the neon miles, Shanghai, Mumbai,
   the full moon trampolining off the continents of ice.

And in the wide blind countryside the lesser fires,
   a thousand isolated signal lamps, a small child's

failing torch, the lonesome phones, a tide
   of phytoplankton clinging to the hull of night.

Such candlepower lit at the shrine
   of darkest space. But is this too much light?

EMERGENCY KIT

In his father's high-grade safety specs
    and nitrile medical gloves in blue,
the child examines the flower-beds,

scientist and superhero in his golden mask
    reaching with his sky-fingers
for the sapling's low blossoms.

These are the very rich hours –
    April, hotter even than forecast,
the parents looking lovingly on.

The adults are packing up to go, have gone.
    The garden's his now in his emergency kit,
all the colours of a new country.

Minute by minute they grow: the boy,
    the tree, the speeding book of hours.

NOT THE PECULIAR WINGS

I have drawn all the plants and flowers very carefully,
from real ones... But I have never seen a fairy
        Cicely Mary Barker, 'Flower Fairies of the Wayside' (1948)

What you love are her knees, sleek
and bony and strong like yours, kneeling
       though not in prayer – listening,

the wings part butterfly, part human skin,
antennae quivering by the flower's mouth:
       White Bindweed, *bellbind, bellweed,*

loudspeaker sounding the end of a war
or the start, a breach in the sea wall,
       at the next junction slight right.

Aged six, you have no idea that she'll live
mostly by scrambling in rail sidings, wrapping
       her beautiful legs round cafe terrace chairs,

that one in five of her wayside classmates
will fail to survive. How could you know
       that the speakers also are listening,

that the wings are pretend but the children
are real, from the school down the road, all of them
       listening for what you do next.

JACK LATELY

has been walking to work, past
the day centre and the Church of Zion
(*There is Hope no matter how fierce
the storm*)
        with a backpack of books,
as many as he can cram in and carry
like an all-you-can-eat deal or delivering
medicines on foot to remote rural areas

because Jack is in training for a long-distance
mountain trail, an ancient route trodden
by soldiers, travellers,
                people used
to carrying their own life-support kit

a path all too easily lost when the weather
moves in with its abominable emptiness
and the unaccountable sound
                of a motorway
like a lost wind off-course and homeless

        despite which Jack still
loves the cloud-shadows, the way
they spill across the fells and pool together
in the inkwells of the tarns
                so that every day
he adds another book, the wherewithal
to survive grown now to the size of a planet –
The Winter's Tale, The Road, La Voix humaine.

MIKA HOWEVER

cannot forget, despite this recent
happiness as a human jukebox
in a beautiful bankside bookshop

– anything a customer would like
a slice of (poetry, crime, Anna's
last scene as the candle goes out) –

and its café where analysts play
the full 3D pocket versions: plains,
dark places, various water bodies.

Does the bee forget the memory
of wax inside the hive?
Do the minnow and the eel forget

the shiver in the water
the night before the quake?

NURSE JAMESON THIRTEEN YEARS ON THE JUVENILE WARD

has seen it all, how they head off down the catwalk
flinging their tiny-booted ankles forward,
eyes shining like engine lamps as the strength

leaks from them like a bandaged tap, something fine
thrown on with just minutes to spare then out
through the walls as if they were water.

And now today this boy in whose body the hope
of adventure still flowers like honeysuckle over a broken wall,
his inexplicable feelings of dread long ago

crammed into the motorcycle glove box
and all the while the scent of peril lifting from him
like smoking rain from the surface of a cliff road.

All behind her now, lost messages in the sand
as she rides her scooter down the miles for home.
There are other things she does to make herself afraid.

LAST DAY ON THE FUTURES FLOOR

It's January. The day's been astronomical
and trader you're the last man on the floor.

The darkened pit's a planetarium where slips
of paper – options, dates – lie crumpled
on the Earth like broken lepidoptera.

You're half asleep and dreaming: at work
in fields near home in summer break
you raise your lengthening arms above your head

and gather down each dripping tassel,
feel the cob-silks brush your aching legs.

Across the world the sun is up.
The markets spike and dip, the orchards
open out their blossoms for the ghosts of bees.

In the fields near home the corn
you'll never touch or see is not yet born.

VISITORS' BOOK

Even the quietest day brings four
    or five: a*mazing to see the actual*
desk/ typewriter/ psychedelia,

      the fingerprints of friends
who came by to drink, the bed like an empty
    church. The place is nothing now

as it was nothing then, an itch
    on a phantom limb, like arriving
too late at a burgled house. Disappointing,

      despite all the words in the book,
every one written in my own fair hand.
      All year it goes on.

WYLDERNESSE

This message is like to be with you
later than I desire.
                          I have entered
a new wilderness – randomly generated
ravines, sunless abysses in the heart
of the financial sector, sirens throughout –
                   and am alone.

Yesterday I climbed the hill
behind the house and went on
over the pass into the next valley,

a realm where not one person
has heard of our village, our rare Eden,
even though it is so close.

I have asked the few strangers I meet
which way is the surest road back
to summer but nobody not one person
                   has the first idea.

O how I would like to be with you,
          how I desire that now.

THE QUIET FRIEND

Delayed by fog, I'm dreaming
     of the place I'm trying to fly from,
my head drooped sideways
     like the victim in a Netflix crime.

I jerk awake: my body thinks
     I must be falling from a tree,
some ancient chip inside that doesn't know
     how far this airport seat is

from a swaying branch – no snakes,
     no birds with their disturbing wings,
no insects quietly tracking
     down the hillsides of my skin.

The Departures bar's still
     crowded with the same souls
arguing the toss, what's wrong, what's right,
     so hard to see, to know.

In any case the final episode reveals
     the truth's the last thing
instinct would have led you to:
     it was the quiet friend all along.

Who could have guessed? The nicest
     person in the neighbourhood,
unthinkable, against all instincts
     in the clever DI's blood.

Outside, the insistent mist: two radio masts
    or else two distant trees.
I might be gone for years. Who knows.
    Maybe I'll never leave.

MAGPIE

Yet another email from Archangel Michael,
slipped through the spam trap like a ghost
through brickwork: *Heaven can help you*
win your breakthrough. Receive it HERE.
I'm afraid to get too much in touch
with Michael patron saint of paratroopers,
but I'd like to see the great green wings
fanned out like the forests of a thousand
emerald knots below me if only I could fly.
You looked so lovely just now, by the way,
the video stream like glass – maybe
a bit subdued, like the lamb as painted
by the famous Spanish master,
its delicate nose that anyone would want
to kiss, its patient stare into the grass.
All I want for my breakthrough
is to crash the force shield of this screen
and be there with you, like the magpie
and the still life, grapes painted so naturally
it tore the canvas with its beak and desperate claws.

THE SKEIN

for Katie and Guy

The skein was the distance between two hands
    looped and taut like sheepswool or flax,
long miles either side of a heartland,
    two lanes running north-south and back –
a migration path, something like birdflight
    but faster than that, heart's data sent high
over farmsteads and factories, coastlands
    and hinterlands, some of it wildcast and lost
till the morning when distance and wingspan
    collapsed like a sail or a linen sheet taken down
out of the wind for folding to bring those hands
    clear touching inches from each other at last.

LANDING STAGE

Dear lady, welcome home.
The Merchant of Venice, Act V, sc i

The wind's unsettled round the jetty,
  steps ashore with us among our skirts.
Water's restless glass is nothing in the hand
but in the hoop of the lagoon's as solid
  as a leaded door. What's in a ring?

Here at the landing stage we stand to meet
  our husbands. With every crossing, something
comes and goes in us, some hidden cargo that we trust
out on the channel. There's no experiment
  to estimate the all we're hazarding.

We take the risk. The night's a deck with us
  held in the hold, the stars small chinks
of daylight through the boards, not gold
but silver, which we settle for. Come morning
  who will be our torch-bearers?

RAIN CHECK

Once I asked if we could take a rain check.
Look at these gathering clouds
I said and you said but that's the nature
of the outdoors
                that even in the belly
of the storm, your clothes clinging
to you like desperate children and down
to your naked bones,
                   that's when
you'll see them, the ringing mountains
    and the water's universe.

And yes some distant voice inside me
did agree
          and so I stood bareheaded
in the rain, alone it seemed, exhausted
on my feet till daylight came,

the returning hour of the shadow-game,
the hour of the blackbird and the wren.

WINDOW

Dear girl, I found your message on the window sill
as I was passing, its folded paper shivering in the breeze
I made. I took it for a moth poised there for flight

but then I read your words, how others say you can't
stand for your rights in heeled shoes, or speak
through painted lips, or do the jobs boys do

which made me look again and see its white sheet
was a handkerchief, not of surrender but farewell,
the old world fading on its blurry way, *goodbye* –

at which I looked again and saw it was a light-filled room
in which like me you've wanted to be everything,
and can and will. I see you at the window now,

the paper wings, the waving hand, the bright expanding room,
and so I leave my note with yours here on the sill
– till soon, your friend and neighbour, World.

THE LONG LOFT

In natural science the principles of truth
ought to be confirmed by observation.
          Carl Linnaeus, *Philosophia Botanica* (1751)

I'd gone up to see where the knocking
was coming from:
                    the long museum loft,
floating like a wide-bodied aircraft
above the kingdomed galleries below

and from whose birds-eye window
across the city's quartered A to Z I saw
how there were other kingdoms too:

the moving and the motionless,
the speaking and the silent,
the kingdoms of the red and blue

and of the yellow with its scattered envoys
everywhere – the trampled primrose,
brimstone in the early butterfly, the orpiment
in ancient glass –
                    first pigment to fade,
lifting off already, pale with February's trace.

I saw then what the knocking in my head might be
and from that date began to order, organise.

CLOSE

She made me pancakes and she gave me gin,
she told me her stories from the road –
their indigo hair, the palaces they lived in –

she spoke to me in a language nearly
but not quite my own like a cloud-show
passing over country several miles away.

She came from the tribe of strangers
and of all the gifts she gave me
the sound of her deep blue mind-cave

is the one I keep pinned to my wall,
like a cutting stolen from the royal hothouses
that can never flower in the real world.

THAT'S HOW THEY FOUND ME

paddling down this rabbit hole of a backwater
because something on my way home from work
had said take to the river, so that even though

I'd put everything in the car (shovels,
provisions for two years), and I'd spent
so long trying to imagine how it would be –

the whole earth alight like a burning star
fallen from heaven, snow climbing
the doorways like a just-landed alien –

there I was just letting the stream take me,
head-torch flashing at the moon, like escaping
over the lake in *A Farewell to Arms*,
crossing the water with nothing but hope.

MY FIRST-RATE FRIEND

Because you swam so hard against the tide,
    the shuttle of its loom, its breaking weave,
and worked alone that night the storm flew
    at your headlamps as you harvested the corn
while the rest of us slept on, and sang
    I don't know if I dreamed this sorry town
or it dreamed me repeatedly

it comes as no surprise to find you here
    gardening in total darkness, sifting earth
to find an inverse kind of air, become
    a plant with leaves, a root, a cliff-top tree,
your lane seen from the moon,
    your house from out at sea.

OUTSIDE THE COLUMBARIUM

For years to ourselves we'd seemed
golden, or fiery red, even green,
all blue being banned by decree,
for saints and the serious, not for you or me.
But the long view shrouded in cloud reveals
that eighty percent of our earthly being is deepening
water, that storms wheel over our heads, wild force-fields
named after girls, unfettered and free,
strange furious birds like feathered machines
raining stones on our chambered turbulent dreams.
I had no idea how blue we would be.

TRYING TO BE REMEMBERED

Lying among leaf-fall he lifts the log or carcass,
presses it toward the sky where happiness
is. What's on his mind is metamorphosis,
himself transfigured, smaller creatures fearless
crawling between his paws, his muscle mass
a fortress, Castle Tenderness, as his roar is.

What in the polished stream he sees is weakness
as something lost or trying to be remembered is.
Meanwhile seasons, then the night itself approaches.
Something forgotten, something from the forest,
snow-fall melting on his pelt, such is
the sight that Beauty lifting the door-latch catches.

They call it betony   appears
in meadows   slopes of cleared
downland   in safe shade
resides   a salve for soul
& body both   a shield
against night-gangers   a plant
of real purity   so gather it
in August only   leave
your ironmongery   at home

Batracion   or sometimes
buttercup   appears in sandy soil
in fields   its thin leaves
few and far between   a remedy
against lune-sickness   wreathed
around the neck   with reddish
thread   beneath a waning
April moon   or in the new days
of October   very very soon
this madness   will be over

The mandrake plant   the great
the glorious *mandragora*   sacred
famed   for its beneficence
come close   you'll know it
by its night-shine   lantern glow
on seeing the head   inscribe it
instantly around with iron   to ground
its flight   from your impure approach
then dig with ivory   till getting
to its hands and feet   you tie them fast

with at the other end   a famished dog
& meat   exactly out of reach
so the hound tugs up   the plant behind
for sleeplessness   & headache
smooth its juice   into the brow
& be astounded   sleep will swiftly
come   & where there's wrongdoing
at home   some clear & grievous harm
take mandrake   to your house's heart
& end for ever   all such evil hurt

For hail & rough winds   turn them
on their heels   with castor flowers
also *ricinus*   hung at home
hung anywhere   will drive back
sleet & squalls   miraculous seeds
hung shipboard   slake the fiercest storms
recite *ricinus*   be thou always in my songs
send hail away   take storms
& lightning from me   in the almighty
name of god   your only maker

BARTHOLOMEW: FOUR THINGS

Of *angels,* their embodiment:
    in flight they are as WINDS
    in prayer as CLOUDS
    also in love as FIRE, the lights that live there
    also as DOCTORS for the healing of the soul.

Of *woods,* their wildness:
    in summer, boughs and branches,
    safe paths marked for strangers
    to the neighbourhood, turned
    and misdirected to the hands of thieves.

Of *doves,* their flight:
    from Syria and Egypt bearing
    word out, no letter without peril
    and for the messages
    they carry, many meeting death.

Of *melancholia,* its darkness:
    within the mouth a taste of earth,
    around the heart a closing-in of sorrow
    – as to the reason for this
    baseless dread, no-one can answer.

CEASELESS TINTINNABULATION

Right now at the limits
        of physics all the circuitry of crickets
and swallows and cicadas
        is gathered in the corridor outside
the lab of the World's Quietest Place
        (minus twenty point six decibels)
waiting to know when they might be heard.

Elsewhere on the planet a bell
        is still ringing behind glass
after one hundred and seventy years,
        oscillating in its sound-proof cell
like a car-alarm buried deep
        in the blizzard. Put your ear to the jar:
not even the trace of a person alone in a room.

One day the glass might crack like the ice
        and we'll get to hear the speech of all
the creatures in the menagerie,
        the unexplained sounds of night.
Till then we must listen for whatever
        we can catch – the glass which is still
ringing, the snow which is still ringing.

NEVERWINTER

Whider trowe this mon has the wey take?/
What road can it be he is walking?
          'The Man in the Moon' – anonymous (fourteenth century)

Our missing train's already in –
Arrived, though not in any world we're in.
Flocks of birds pass by like fields
at a carriage window. The sun goes down
behind the warehouses, fantastic city in ruins.

We lift our faces to the moon, to the man
halted there forever with his burden
on the road to legendary Stormreach,
Neverwinter, Shadowguard. World
without end, still so far from home.

She's sixty metres below me in the castle's inner courtyard, my other self, where the sun only reaches for a few weeks in summer. I could abseil down now to her past the finials and corbels and she'd tell me how safely she's keeping my heart there in the shade: it's OK she'd say, it's floating like a baby in the finest brandy inside its crystal casket, just like the hearts of Richard Coeur de Lion and Eleanor of Castile.

And I can see it, trailing its translucent ribbons like a deep-sea fish, ready for immediate transport across no matter what terrain, accompanied by fire-wagons against attack by wolves. Meantime, its space here in my chest is filled with flowers and salts and spices, and I'm content to wait here on the battlements looking out to sea, watching for your return.

GREAT-STREAM-OF-THE-WORLD

Place of the cutty grass
Place of the listening post

   Path like a long white cord

I in a small boat hand-carved
navigating by the stars and sun toward you

   one island to another

Place of the standing cloud
Place of the tussock grass

   (may be translated differently)

I overland on the long treks out
from all the bus depots toward you

   Something ghostly about you now

Place of the umbilicals
I by air above the mounds of cloud toward you

   Something about distance about cloud

About how to translate anything

THE AIR STILL

The air still, the step down
easy
        from the soaked hem
of the water-meadow
behind the sports centre

then twelve thousand miles
without breaking stroke

a clear stretch through the calm
green waters of proxemic theory,
        measurements made
with parts of the body.

So many others also in the water.

Aound three a.m. the rip-tide hours.
Many small islands. Then first light

on the reclaimed foreshore
        six hundred metres
from the slip-road to your door.

A DAY BY THE SEA AND OTHER STORIES

...c'était une partie de son être qui avait fini d'exister
        En famille, Guy de Maupassant

The windows of the tram car were open
and all the curtains floated in the wind.
I love this book because you gave it to me,
short stories you're too young to understand.

The door opened and Dr Chenet appeared.
On this near-deserted beach I think of you
at home beside the window, practising
on the cracked piano that I learned on too.

The windows of the tram car were open.
I swim alone now on a glittering tide
of doctors, clocks and chests of drawers,
gas lamps, free-floating globes of light.

I love this book because you gave it to me.
He thought of his mother in Picardy, just
as she was when he was a boy. Recognisable
people and what happened to them next.

THE EXPERIMENT

Dearests I have arrived. Some things
have already been taken: the small blue bowls
and airmail stationery, the summer tablecloth (only
slightly blue), and the half-light is now quite cleared.

All I can say is, try when you come not to think
of the dark: take the boat and do the experiment –
you will have to put every ounce of what you know
into it or it will never lift off or be carried across.

In a small country like ours you must be prepared
for no-one to think this possible, like the first pioneers
of flight those two so close all their lives, watching the wind
and birds, their dazzling feats and equilibrium.

Sleep is chalky now. Most of the underblue
has gone from beneath the bed. Only the light remains
and the roses wild and idle just as you will remember them.
Stay together whenever the times allow.

ACKNOWLEDGEMENTS

Thanks are due to the following publications in which some of these poems were first published in print or online: *Bath Magg, The Hippocrates Book of the Heart* (eds. Wendy French, Michael Hulse and Donald Singer, Hippocrates Press 2017), *Napkin Poetry Journal, Oxford Magazine, Oxford Review of Books, Pestilence* (eds. Peter Pegnall and Gérard Noyau, Lapwing 2020*), Poetry Ireland, Poetry London, Poetry Wales, Stephen Spender Prize, TLS* and *Write Where We Are Now* (MMU 2020).

'Landing Stage' is a revised version of a poem commissioned for performance as part of the *Shakespeare Liturgy: The Merchant of Venice,* 2019.

'Window' was written as part of the CSSG (India) 'And Still I Rise' project, 2017.

'Extracts from the Old English Herbarium' is an extracted translation from the eleventh-century *Old English Illustrated Herbal and other medical remedies* – British Library Cotton MS Vitellius C II.

'Bartholomew: Four Things' is an extracted translation from *On the Properties of Things,* 1397, a vernacular translation by John Trevisa of *De Proprietatibus Rerum* (Bartholomeus Anglicus, Paris, thirteenth century).

The translated Māori place names in 'Great-stream-of-the-world' are taken from the Aotearoa New Zealand government website https://nzhistory.govt.nz.

My warm thanks are owed to Alice, Anne and Morten, and Caroline and David for their generous kindness in offering me such lovely places in which to work. Also to all the Helyar poets – Fiona Benson, Patrick Brandon, John Wedgwood Clarke, Julia Copus, Claire Crowther, Carrie Etter, Annie Freud and Jenny Lewis – for their irreplaceable poetic friendship and advice, which I'd be lost without. Finally but by no means least, heartfelt thanks to Michael Schmidt and to John McAuliffe for his invaluable editorial guidance and unstinting encouragement.